forget thee
Copyright © Ian Dreiblatt, 2021

ISBN 978-1-946433-75-6
First Edition, First Printing, 2021

Ugly Duckling Presse
The Old American Can Factory
232 Third Street #E-303
Brooklyn, NY 11215
www.uglyducklingpresse.org

Distributed in the USA by Small Press Distribution
Distributed in the UK by Inpress Books

Cover art by Andrew Steinmetz
Design and typesetting by Doormouse
The type is Baskerville

Books printed bound at McNaughton & Gunn (Saline, MI)
Cover printed offset at Prestige Printing (Brooklyn, NY)

The publication of this book was made possible, in part, by a grant from the National Endowment for the Arts, by public funds from the New York City Department of Cultural Affairs in partnership with the City Council, by the support of the New York State Council on the Arts, with the support of Governor Andrew M. Cuomo and the New York State Legislature. This project is supported by the Robert Rauschenberg Foundation.

forget thee

ian dreiblatt

for Mieczysław

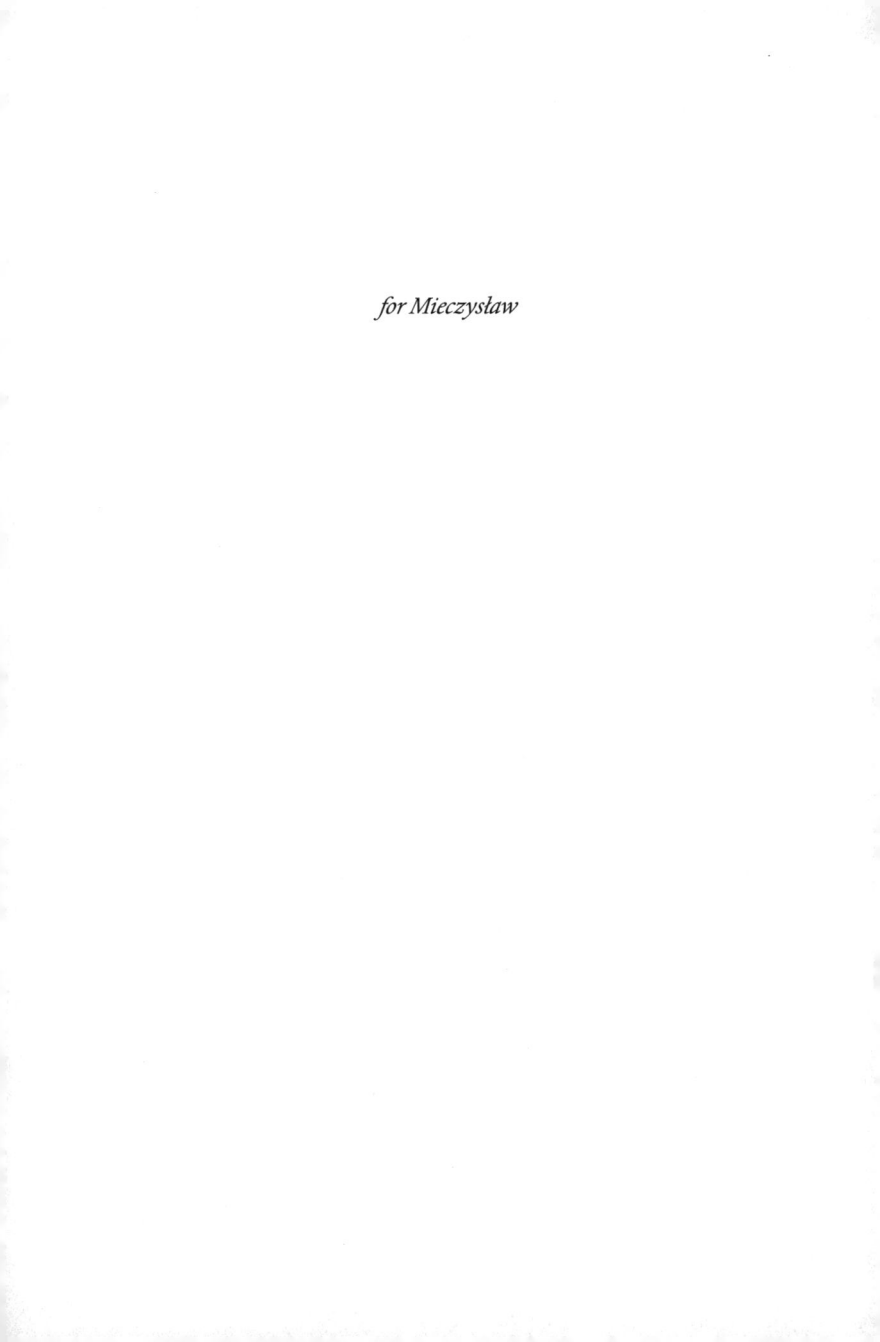

<u>dunjaluče</u>

I hope you got some cool mountain air tonight

glamping with you is better even than sharing a coke

I hope you are setting a new record for summer coziness
in a sufi commune on an old shaker farm

on the bus ride home the divinity of travel blurred into
the divinity of habitation until I became fleetingly translucent

well what are saints for if not to break the distance between the things around us and the words we use

breach sonata, the highway is the radio is or weather or
even news tho the news is bad we feel and say so much
and can never understand this sweetness of all language

lately when I travel in the u.s., I imagine each state is
its own country, as tho that had happened and we'd all
survived it

tho in fact survival is allocated under terms we detest and
the roads are full of holes aching

still new york state has some of the most beautiful woods
how lovely are thy tents et cetera

in brooklyn a subway is becoming a pokéworks

the canal where that dolphin died and I texted Joseph
and he put it in a poem is steaming from its green glassy
surface

there's an army of poets here who carry poetry instead of
money wear poetry instead of clothes occasionally throw
each other down staircases and

if you're not listening to the 6-minute 12-inch dance mix
of *walk like an egyptian*, you're totally missing the song

this weekend Ada said to us you'd be good to be friends
with in a genocide

she remembered passing into north american life as the
phrase *ethnic cleansing* was passing into english

and how during that war the litanies of strife summoned
danger and you might swap your coffee with someone in
case it was poisoned

not because you more deserved it, but to lay a claim on
the power of allocation

decide to share even violence

which is everywhere losing its shame

there are minor poetries but as Daša Drndić says there
are no minor fascisms

or there is minor art but no minor politics

the weak universalism of the avant-garde dreams a sign
of victory that recedes ever deeper into the other part of
sleep

we know all kinds of buildings

we speak darkness backwards into the heart we're waiting
to hear about in hospitals lofts salvaged from industry
crumbling houses salvaged from capital

in turkish *saray* means *palace* a word the northern slavs of
russia twisted mockingly to mean *shack* and the southern
slavs of bosnia borrowed for their capital

at least that's what Bella told me one day, that they called
their shacks palaces in turkish and learned to thread the
steppe with iodine

while we walked around the bronx and talked about not
getting the simpsons

Himzo Polovina sings a song about sarajevo, I can't pronounce it but it's *dunjaluče golem ti si golem ti si* means *you are enormous* and *dunjaluk* means *the mortal, material world*, a saeclum that can solvet

from the arabic *dunya* and the turkish *luk* and the form *dunjaluče* means the world is being spoken to

tho in fact we've mostly forgotten a world can be spoken to

the psychiatrist sets chairs around a table

hello world I am speaking to you now the soft science of contact or mystery of convection

hello world you're going to want to sit down for this

the world idea walks like a crab into the heart of a greasy pond

Maria writes that she's seen a big, windowless paddywagon in the streets, very high-tech and it worries her

when harm looks to the sky the stars it sees are different

chattering teeth, victrola amid rubble, knife buried under a hill

between what we know we know and what we can bear to think we know homesick for a world culture that has never come into being

hey world you're wide and you're hot and you've fed me a lot

woodward avenue simply beautiful the empty bullring pastoral

hey world you calamitous thrillbox you zoetrope of glamours and subversions you bear in garbage city

hey world distinct from the infinite I think I found some infinity here despite you

the psychiatrist carries a lute and when one day he dies everyone will ask what the last song he sang was

you and Ada and Rachael caught in the red light on the hill by the fire this was real life only days ago

we stopped for egg sandwiches totally yolkadelic

later alone at night in a tent on a mountain ulterior economies pool in our happiness

a frog gets in

treat every earthling as an invitation to gentleness

down the hill and past the fields, buildings of every description, cars piloted by lunatics

a juice shop with four options wake up green monster for you hippocrates

the windowless paddywagons grunt down alleys unseen

I guess I mean to say we are homesick for meaning

harm clothes itself in bare aesthetics (in the pleasured air, Peter Dimock says), sic transit vocoder off the side road

later still your words gather at the bus window like real breath

in 1565 Ivan the Terrible created a new force for the allocation of violence

he called them the oprichnina, men who rode in black cloaks like monks, carrying severed dogs' heads and brooms

(to sniff out rebellion and sweep it away)

oprichnina means "the widow's share," that a greater politics has died, the sovereign that was its wife laying claim to some remainder

the police inhabit every affect

mere enforcement is loosed on the world

and anyone will drink rather than go thirsty

bastards will steal even your grief if they can get it

hey world there's no definition of violence we all agree on

or can untangle from a more basic idea of what living is

hey mortal, material world, you are enormous

a tear opens up in the fabric of scarcity and a thousand tissue paper flowers fly out

run from bee mistaken for frolic heaven's on fire et cetera

the brittle joy of being finite is to end and to begin

thank you to verbs for everything you do

thank you to whatever it was sand or water or shade that kept time

the bus pulls in and I walk to the train, city at its usual polyrhythm

it's hard to find a name for the experience of caring about people in a time of totally cockamamie civilizational collapse an age of dog's heads and brooms

mostly I just wish you were here and hope you come to an agreement with the moths

I settle in among zany hummus flavors and oprah clips, we have everything in the city

the horizon bends across a night sky to touch you

as for everything that's happened so far, if we cannot retrace it

after all the forgetting that language requires

utopianism's yelp page will be hearing from me

the lightfoot hears you and the brightness begins
across a yard of blossoming yucca and
opuntia
      storm in the distance
what do we do?
                we sit here, replaying the death of
buildings. roll back. sprung crocodilopolis,
rock we pretend is literal
overtaking time. I was an owner of donkeys
and an owner of ploughlands, before the harsh
age
     ideology a boombox perched on
the lip of a volcano

welcome to   enormous pink
trees dudes with giant beards academy of
scorpions
                and every morning
you talk and talk you say the same thing so that
a city rises up inside you   our
social entanglements become a horizon
that meaning disappears against
        up for the down
of whatever an after is
                & when what's ending
is over you'll be amazed the things you miss
eternal color of windex
sound of one or another floor

walk into the sphere
the video to something to
talk about playing endlessly
on a glass cube in a glass
room
    crystal archive gets the
world
    something to talk
about winged chariot something
to talk about stink machines, human
mass rummaging thru core code as
it dials down to make every
circle a sympathetic
zero
    something to talk about not
knowing how to know anything,
sad alluvium calculus piling on
our shores
       something
to talk about your neighbor in
the street and bleeding

apocalypse party everyone
in the pool you came from
a house but forget the house
you had a language once but
forget the
        language
      speak in sand

                        speak in the
recognition of marvels, endless
sentences
                archive
light as the dark sky
settles
                sure I remember the
world it seethed with cartels it
ate its own morning

I conjure Narām-Sîn, the
twenty-third-century-bce
akkadian king, and
take him for a walking
tour of new york city

what, he asks, are
these mighty ziggurats? o,
I tell him, they're market
places selling combustion
to ghosts in a
magnetized steam of
currency, and what
do they do with
the currency, he
asks, and I say, all
kinds of things but
a big portion goes to
harming their
enemies and wrapping
bacon around things

who are their enemies,
he asks, & I say, none of
us met a shadow we
couldn't spite, we shamed
the very sky into
nearness

then Narām-Sîn the
third-century-bce
akkadian king asks,
what are these brown
rock-like things & these
greenish earth
phalluses, these we
call potatoes, I say,
and hot peppers they're
fantastic

so we cook them
up he loves
them, whoa these are
great it would be a
shame to lose a world with
potatoes and hot
peppers and what I think
is maybe you should
just focus on this if you
want my opinion

Julius Caesar enters
the room ancestral
spirits bending the
window's light like
a pool, linen meshed
with metals, and then
gravely speaks, I was a
swinger of metals and
a bender of spirits I
killed so many people
they named a
month after me

my city outlast the earth
my every war sacred
my will the partition
of bounded from
infinite

            feed me mice
and spaghetti

I say to Julius Caesar,
that's a tall order but
can I get you anything
else, & he's like, yes bring
me the sky's blood as a
sign in the name of my
empire   ok

                    Julius
Caesar briefly invents
lightning, he sighs, before
me nothing was
final I broke the morning
in two, so I frown &
tell him about chase
scenes in the movies &
how everyone has a
second face growing out
the back of their
head & about internet
chat-rooms

me I'm simple, he
says, I like killing
lots of people & then
shitting in the
woods, and he
grins adding, oh grow
up that's politics

now I am in ancient
egypt with the prophet
Jeremiah. is it weird,
I ask, to be a prophet?

no it just means they
haven't burned what
you wrote, he says

I came from a
lineage of priests in
a small northern
town, we had a
sacred mailbox, all
the sheep of
happiness everything

we moved to the city
which is awful got
work as priests an
impossible situation we'd
be reading the most
beautiful ancient shit,
that to be in any world
is also an exile our songs the
sleeping of bridges, all this
super beautiful shit,
while they slit screaming
goats' necks thru the

window divine right
of goat's blood everywhere

and then bastards came
the incoherence in their
teeth an ache that
only dominion could fill

so we fled here to
the birthsite of
difference, to make
cities of ourselves,
a tiny temple wherever
any two words meet

what would you do all
day, I ask? I'd write, he
says, or dictate to
my friends, I
mastered the law of
phantomed bodies, learned
to unspool whatever
tongues knew

I cast red fabric from
the library windows and
tried to make an intimacy
between my memory
and the memory of

the world only it turns
out worlds don't remember
a goddamn thing

poetry is hard work, I
say! & he's like, yeah
poetry is hard work

what did you write, I
ask? o what does
it matter? I sided with
kings, priests, teachers, I
picked allies &
causes in rooms I
dreamt a deep sleep of
pure listening &
carried back what
I could, none of this
makes sense now, here, I
am a different person

you sound depressed, I
say, not really, he tells me, I
worked the braids of
circumstance as best
I could, the air & how
to fill it, I lived a life of
art & besides someone had
to do something, us

just living there in
the desert, so much
past & so little history

I walk up the
western shore
of manhattan with
Puabi, mysterious
noblewoman of
twenty-seventh-
century-bce
mesopotamia

what are these
giant metal teeth
rising out of the
earth, she asks, I've
never seen so
much metal? these
are monuments, I
say, and she's like,
to who? to the
idea that the city
makes at least some
kind of sense

and these torn
shimmering husks
that blow through
your streets, she
asks? I say, oh
we loved a gurgling
nut water made
from a reconstruction

of what grain is, we
bought it in these
cylinders drank its
angelic specificity while
a ghost of our
heartbreaks was
continuously
resculpted in the
public consciousness,
it became the single
easiest thing in
the world to get

she looks at the
skyscrapers and
laughs, these wildly
erect stone shaftways a
little on-the-nose don't
you think, & I'm like,
sure but we don't love
to talk about that

where do you
live, she asks,
and I say, in an
interconnected
nest of paper
compartments
within the
towers   wild

I draped topaz over
the doorposts and
heard my name
transposed into
weeping blue
atlas cedar, I had
conversations with
violence itself,
armies lurching in
my throat, & slept
on linen in a stone
house in a world
that had already
survived I did ok

ok, I say, but
you didn't know
what lightning
was we sent our
faces beaming into
hands we loved
from out above
the sky, yeah, she

says, and you lived
in a giant stone
dick diorama, and
didn't know what
lightning was either

in the end I
wore jewelry as
beautiful as actual
leaves had 50
people bashed to
death in my
honor the height
of elegance

do you still do
that for rich
people, she
asks? I say,
basically, and
she's like good
good one only
has so much time
and anyway we all
need something
to look forward to

I sit down with
Hathor in a cruddy
diner in new jersey

I was embarrassed, I
tell her, to
accidentally see thru a
neighbor's window the
big wonderful rainbow
painted over a wall

think how the sky
feels, she says,
and becomes a cone
of incense then a
snake then a sega
genesis finally
a cow, then she
adds, ask for what
you need we don't
understand what you
want from us

I want another kind
of language, I say, houses
have eyes and I don't
understand how anything
means anything at all —

Hathor laughs happily, no
no human ever
has, & we never meant
to pretend we had answers,
who can say where
to draw the line between
scholarship and
theft, why the
shreds of articulation
blow thru you like a
sandstorm?

                that's right,
I say, we know only
that we're near each
other somehow, stranded
in experience, doing
world in hope of sweetness

doesn't sound half-bad,
she says and I answer, well
it is & it isn't — oh, she
interrupts, oh I know I
know I know I know

she says it reassuringly
then turns into a
flaming carnelian then a
can of spaghetti-os then a
sycamore tree then a

woman mid-forties with
a hat that contains the
sun and has cow horns

you flowerers in every
corruption, she says,
you leakiest vocabularies
of commune, you
etymologies whose blood
is food for pavement,
I may love humanity but
of *course* I'd rather
be a cow on a riverbank

yeah, I tell her, we
know, our walls peeling
with rainbows into air
wet with sirens, our
criminal breath the
last thing beautiful,
once you start reading
you can never go
back and I cannot
stress enough
how little sense it
all makes

she throws the sun from
her head and it falls
behind a jukebox, says,

I know, being anyone
is an exhausting
coincidence for you,
all we invented was
forests and the musical
body

      to be fair, I
tell her, we never
know what we're
doing, we just slosh
down liquids and
decline to stop talking

she turns into a
lion then a painted
sandstone column
then the color
orange then a
1991 honda civic

this is so you
guys, Hathor says,
no god could think
up automated
shoulderbelts or the
feeling of an outdoor
movie, vibe
committee to
sector earth, and that's

what I like about
you, she throws in, even
as the last atari
sun grinds still in
the sky, you're all
just lined up, in
ridiculous clothes,
waiting to have
feelings that
change you again

I open my
eyes & see
Geshtinanna, sister
of wine, standing
there

hi how are
you, I say? I
am not good, she
tells me, my brother
Dumuzid married the
goddess Inanna, one
day she came
home from hell with
a flock of demons Dumuzid
hardly noticed & just
said hi, he was watching
some dancers but really,
who doesn't say whoa
demons! & so

Inanna got mad & had
him dragged to
hell in her place, now
he's dead which means I
have to keep watch over
the earth half the year while
everything goes to
shit because only
he can bring flower honestly

would it have killed him
just to say wow demons?
anyway how are you

I'm fine, I say, the ocean
hasn't stopped its
music in sixty trillion
years and we found a
way to make illness
into a tiny animal tell
me more about your brother

what's to tell? he dies &
comes to life again, every
year, they'll argue what

it means, how he's like
anyone else who dies &
comes back they'll
ask if he was a king, was
dismembered, if he was
a raiser of ghosts, the
hand that plucked the
string of the sea

no one gives a
shit about the dry
season or torture but
when you wake up one
morning & you're a

cactus I'll be off getting
high with the north
star or something
and we'll just see
how you like it

"oxen wild like bellowed land"

after most things have happened, Chaon appears.
he's filth, a mishmash theophage guzzling chaos

out of the city, draining it to linearity. doors become
invisible, alphabets realign their orders under the

meshes of our speech. I will mutely scowl says the sun.
I will turn the chrysler building inside out.

he drank so much chaos they called him Chaon,
of course. he took all but two of every household

(as though walls even existed, or remembered light)
and lived in the sky with them. open air pivoting,

invisible embouchure into a body of contradictions.
or into nobody if that's who we are. I was righteous

out of my age, says Chaon. I soldered together
the seams of the sky, I blew breath into the city's

gridded syntax. weeks without rain. flesh in no
number. recombinant grammars flash in the

skyline. the doorway. a language all breath
conspires in. bandwidths enlacing to form noise.

Thoth the ancient
egyptian god of
wisdom who is
also a white-haired
baboon and
sometimes an ibis
walks lankily over

I will be honest, he
tells me, because that's
how I am I have read
what you're doing
it doesn't make
sense to me

o is that all, I ask? me
either but I power
thru, nothing really
makes sense like
ever, the air full
of imaginary
money and some
people own music
or own medicine,
our bodies breaking
into pieces all
around while we
just fight about the
right way to fall or
be taken apart

I've seen you do it,
Thoth says, even
gave you writing so
you'd have another
kind of body to
escape to, and you
hid everything there,
your inquiries into
love, rules for making
particular kinds of
soups, everything
you know about what
glass does to light,
where to put hands
in the dark, your
fears and memories
of an earlier landscape

you made all your
houses out of writing,
every number has an
asshole and the
numbers and the
assholes you converted
to writing, tree and
door, propeller jet
and dim glow of
minerals, all of this
you concealed within
the endless conceptual

folds of the writing
I gave you

still, I say, we managed
a lot — you could
live in the woods and
get jewelry brought
by uniformed agents
of the state, and there
were stations where
people sold pizza and
explosive oil from
underground vats
thru a big rubber
proboscis. it made
no sense and we
loved it. the days
felt electric. music
became razor-like. plus
old fruit makes you
dizzy because ps
you're a monkey
life really wasn't bad

and you, I ask, what
did you spend that
time doing? I did so
much, he says, got
married to equilibrium,
gathered all the

ink I could, tried my
best to relate to
you but there was
no body any of
you would stay
put in

you loss that
perceives

we look back
over the hills
and Thoth gets
sad, in a way, he
says, this is all
my fault, writing
is the gift you
didn't survive

but we achieved so
much, I tell him: pinball, the
poems of Bernadette
Mayer, the music of
Lonnie Johnson, frozen
pirogi, little rooms that
glide between mountains

for a little while, he
says, sure, I mean I
used to be the freaking moon

but you don't hear
me bragging about it

pejorocracy it's an insane process
cacaphonocracy the billboards tuned
to full bleed radiocracy the country of
your heart corporocracy its bodies
bound by vacant interests you know
normal boilerplatocracy. leocracy.
guacamocracy how are things in
the digital surround right now?

cryptocrats take forever in the bathroom.
we try to make a book to the exact
dimensions of our complicity

Cleopatra obviously is
awesome & I'm excited
to meet her in the
transtemporal blank
space between the tops
of four pyramids

I was queen to a loving
people, she tells me, a tamer
of bees a surge in the stream
of tradition

what did you do for
fun, I ask her? drank
actual milk with actual
honey in it in the shade
by a river, she tells me,
is it any wonder our
preoccupations were
with paradise?

let it be said I had
a lot to lose, Cleopatra
tells me, I learned to
talk to brewers and
soldiers, pulled catfish
from the river, I married
my brother like any
reasonable person drank
the sapphire tears of the

desert. do people still
come out of their bodies
as birds & fly into the
sun? do they still fuck
on flat stones next to
statues of cats? are
watermelons
           still
tiny? do gods still
love onions? who makes
your bread

watermelons are huge, I
tell her, & our bread is made in
tremendous workshops by
spiritless beings who
speak in geometry

do you have a queen, she
asks, no just a
succession of crazed
viziers who stand
around eating candy all
day & absconding ever
deeper into cutaway
diagrams of their own
urethras. happens all the
time, she tells me, happens
to the best of us.

      a mountain for
president, a falcon for
president we don't feed
gods anymore we eat
them, I say, I understand
perfectly, Cleopatra replies

you think I don't know
what you're going thru? I
collaborated with a
foreign power, I a handmaid
to imperium, I, who walked
flowering sands, left my
country forever after
captive, our crowns
disappearing out of the
actual earth — that is some
end-of-history shit, let
me tell you

at least we both lived while the
pyramids stood, I say, and had
no idea what existence is

and Cleopatra scowls, what's
all this we stuff you
mortal motherfucker

I go out for a burger
with Nebuchadnezzar
II he loves our clever
meat shapes alien
crackle of our streets

he tells me, I once
had a man's sons
killed in front of
him immediately
before blinding him
forever with a
hot sword, do we
never learn to
pick out the subtle
patternings that
resonate through us?

we gather them
into huge metaphors,
I tell him, and sell
those, when our
market couldn't
accommodate them
we built a new market,
I understand, he tells
me, there are many
realities, and one
can build a market in
any of them

I laid bricks out on
my name until people
were living inside it,
bruised distances
blotting the hills,
let history remember
me in flames I did not
give one solitary shit

and what about the
tower in your city, I ask? he
says, fuck the tower
and the city and the
long ivory carvings in
the treasury house and
the view of the
river, fuck everything
that wants to subdue
the great kerosene elbow,
look I'm not pretending
to know anything I
just say err on the side
of burning all this shit to ash

cut yourself and a
question oozes out,
shore of the red question
blaze extincted of answer

we swallow intricate
gems, I say, that scramble
us the clouds rain
torches on our command

I understand, he tells
me, there are many
realities and one
can fight a war in
any of them

then he pauses and
adds, what can I
say I'm a romantic it's
great to be alive

1961 Malcolm X on tv   he looks hungry
signal fades, angles project a head to
watch it snow thick analog fuzz over
let my arm forget let me be all the people
in this city

        the faucet's running

                gestures of
language vibrate off into permanent
luminous blocks

        walls of vhs wobble rise up
a voice bleeds from a sequence of rectangular
lights that impersonates a tree

                it is our
pleasure to serve you

        it is already late
our sense of what's happening absconds
into figuration

        embarrassed at not
knowing arabic

        at naming our parents
after the little house on that mountain
the music stops

        a rock falls
from the sky and we just go crazy
for it

    faces coalescing from the high-speed
ambient flicker of medium grid and dissipating
back into it

        which the city does, too

arriving as brief rushes of language
& then cubing back off into
predicament
     & as for the ones who
brought us here
       let knives tear their
alphabet
   let it rot
      the mouths of
their children
     while speech, depolarized
as a matter of sovereignty,
         swells
against the contours of absence

I am walking with
Augustus the first
roman emperor by
the tiber as night
falls like an apple

he's smoking a
marlboro a habit
it is hard to imagine
him forming and
he walks with a swivel

glancing up from
the graffiti he says,
I like what the
kids are doing my
eyes in springtime
just tell me
what or who is
Michael Jackson

long story, I tell
him, but for a few
years once the
milky ocean gave
us a perfect child
until horror like a
tide arose as it
does and we realized
we'd been dancing

to the rapture
of our end
jagged twirl endless
falsetto a stranger
to sleep

he squints I play
him *beat it* but
he hates that, what
is this noise about? o,
I tell him, it's about
soldiers meeting in
the square and about
the space in our
minds where no god lives

gods, he says, I do
not care my father
was a god and I'm a
god-to-be, my name
the bloody knife
of peace give me
something better

so I play him *21st
century schizoid
man* by king
crimson which he
also hates but at
least finds engaging,

what is this the
sound of, he asks
and I say, it's
an attempt to reclaim
the sap of a half-
remembered tree

I used to think about
that kind of
thing, he says, but
it never matters
you're born in
a stable, you ride
around in boats,
kill your father's
friends, feed queens
to a snake. what's
to remember? every
minute tells you
how to live, that's
what music is

so I play him
temperature by Sean
Paul and he gets
excited, finally
temple music I
who love life love
this and all things holy

and time *is* cold
why do you think
lovers in the middle of
a town stand so still?

you don't seem
troubled by much,
I tell him and he's
like, eh life's ok I
opened my eyes
one day and
people just started
bringing me peaches
the alien maths of
divinity blossom
wherever I point my
finger and I am
one of the
cleanest people
who've ever lived

it's a joke to be
anybody in my
case the joke was
pretty good

does that mean you
were happy, I ask? &
he says, it means the
world was a tally of

my accumulations that
crumbled as it neared
completion, that I
endured pain but not
suffering and fucked
the very earth in
marble, that I abstained
from nothing but
bad taste while every
year the sun
rebirthed itself what
    kind of a
question is that?

I can't understand
anything, I tell
him, we dreamt
of an adventuring
plumber a rabbit
who feeds you
sugar we took
photos of photos
of photos until
ground gave way
to medium, the
mountain turned from
us to hide its
bruises and we
never stopped
punching, is there

no way for a culture
to take a rest?

the rest, he tells me,
is the imperial repose
of power in its
dispersion: the tensile
distance, your constant
enlacement in a
pliant network,
the courage to call
bloodshed pacification

and then, I ask? and then
nothing, have a smoke,
play music, spend the
night singing in a
cursed palace, whatever
it takes you to
finally fall asleep finally
fall asleep fall asleep
asleep asleep to finally
finally fall asleep

we have heard of the pride of MOAB.
he is very proud,
even of his haughtiness, and his pride, and his arrogance,
his factless boasting.

and so MOAB wails for MOAB,
every one will wail, stung bitterly,
will mourn the baked sweets from that city of feminine sun.

for the fields that feed the city of invention languish,
and the famous vines of the city of fragrance,
whose gardens have proved greater
than the lords of whole peoples;
they reached other towns to the east,
they meandered into the wilderness;
their branches spread wide,
passing over the sea.

so I will weep along with those eastern lands
for the burned vine of that city.
I will water you with tears,
city of invention, and city of rising to the sky,
you whose fruits, whose harvests
are curdled in a cry for war.

happiness and joy are taken
out of that green field,
and the vineyards are empty of song.
no shouts in the air, no wine in the presses,
I have quieted the shouting vintage.

like a harp my heart moans for MOAB,
my guts for the city of feminine sun.

or like picture a burned-
out street still tender from
flame, steam darkening stone
walls & the old woman walking
down it clothes torn spitting at
people is Wisdom

she doesn't like the
food here, the shitty
electric twilight, drone
rangers coursing beyond
the stone wall

she walks into the library
it is much too quiet to think
here where is all the
language? we make a kind of
little boat out of tree-
paper, I tell her, & darken
it in richly detailed patterns.
do the patterns repeat,
she asks? yes & there
are untold millions of
them, swapping code thru
the deep computational
occlusions, hearing &
mishearing themselves &
each other & the terrible
centuries

what are these infinite
twinkling squares, Wisdom
asks? o, I say, we invented
a kind of writing made of
smaller writing & then the
argument whether
it's alive or not

perfectly flat screens
the air around them
viscous flicker in
search of a signal

Wisdom touches
a gas tower and it
explodes, and who
keeps the tablets
or the hyper-dissolution
drive or the holy
index card, & I'm
like, o we dismembered
whatever law we
had & spread its
parts around the
world

Wisdom is really
pissed, that's the fucking
end of it you fucks I'll
feed you cigarettes who

watched my hair burn

I smash the collars
of interlacing system
I seed your shores with
poisonous abstraction
I piss in all your
reservoirs I eat your
knowledge & drink the
empty space where
knowledge used to be

I shit on your lunch
in the mass calorie
depot I flood your
streets with vinegar &
drunk-dial the
ocean while fire takes
the city invert agriculture
so it feeds only the dead I
condemn your mouths to
endless fainting prayer I
poison the numbers as you're
trying to count them I get
your kids into van halen &
teach your country to
love airshows

but Wisdom, I say, life
is in fact so beautiful that

mostly we just walk around
feeling like assholes all
the time, you wouldn't even
understand, our metaphors
for how night follows morning
make us *weep*

& the time I birth will
eat the color out of
ruins, she answers, & mummify
your seas in plastics. it will
coat your science in oil in a
field of writhing storks. it will
say knock you out, bowl
you under, unmoor medicine
from its diseases, it will not
even burp after absorbing the
totality of what has
happened

when the eclipse finally
comes we're so fatigued by
public speech that we're
ready to believe there *is*
no eclipse, just a conversation
about an eclipse that
we have to be trapped in for
it to have meaning, we
fall back into cascading
negatives, wet our hair
in non-being then step
outside to meet the
state

what is there left to
exaggerate?

           well a
lot somehow, but

think back, when I was in
the fifth grade we had
to take part in a mandatory
chorus class where
we sang Billy Joel's *we
didn't start the fire*, in
which time is an inferno,
set farther back than
memory, growing closer
& engulfing us

Billy Joel only put out
one more single, r*iver
of dreams*, a duet with
color me badd in which
he completes a career-
long voyage deep into
a forest conveniently
lush with symbols.
it is here that Billy Joel
absconds fully into dream, a
dust-funked bladescape,
centuries of
cultural accumulation
building up inside us
like silt and I am
only two-thirds joking

a world that saw
the sun disappear
while Billy Joel poured
from the speakers of
a patriotically-themed fried
chicken truck in
a country at war in
a city of tiger-lilies
and nightsticks

yeah I lived there

we had to eat every
book ran thru canals
waving the remainders
of light dusk of the
whole endless accretion
of dusks & way up high
in his obelisk Billy Joel
starting the fire and were we
asking to be consumed

I am sitting by a river
with Enheduanna the
first poet known to
history by name from
the 2200s bce

she wants to know what
people say in unison now,
oh, I tell her, we have more
parallax than unison, since the
big empty fractaled off into
infinite micronothings, she
nods, that's why we started
writing things down, and
by the way it was wonderful
like waking in a fresh
body each morning

and what do you sing into?
she asks, I say, history I
guess or the ability to sign a
timeline what about you? and
she says, a dream of a woman
young and full of power
her great awesomeness
covers the great mountain
and levels the roads

she raises floods clothes
herself in whirlwinds

speaks a hot language
that melts amethyst
out of the earth

what do you do all day,
she asks me and I say, oh
mostly reconfigure small
columns of light into finely-
tuned looping patterns and
then worry about various
aspects of the loops, what
about you?

it varied, sometimes
washing stone feet
sometimes chanting until
you felt like a
marionette one day I
had the thought *could
writing be a medium for
poetry* but then again
who can live in a body
someone else made them
and how long might
any language keep et cetera

except then I tried it & it
worked I wrote poems
down and could feel
them scratching across

the translucent
surface I became of
a smooth red tablet

oh, I say, well we took
things a little far maybe
we threaded the world
with infinitesimal writing
the air our bodies the
shores of the continents

she says, all any world
ever was is whatever you
miss from it, the streets'
shifting intimacies, smells
of friends' houses, outcroppings
of rock, ghost and commodity

so write it all down,
she says, write it in stone
in the loose morning
of nothing we hoped for
ten thirty sits like a
diamond and you'll
never believe this but
that's all there ever
was anyway

the thundermakers descend.

over time, you forget things, a
shadow flickers and disappears out
of the richness of what's happened.

the whole complex of human
relations coming loose or drowning,
or encrypting itself into a new
dialect, my little room alive
with accidental voices, Nick
DeBoer says red night
antimatter, Samuel Delany
says cultural fugue, Tracie
Morris says a dark-matter
eco-experience, Robert Duncan
says something had intruded, a
higher reality
                wherever we
have a we to speak we're a
spell against mischief, the
pulse of measures in last
things. Alice Notley says,
I entered a cave for seven
years not even accessible
to daniels dreams.

in a spherical room, a tube of
light plays don't go chasin'
waterfalls alongside a

nanoscreen explaining what
waterfalls were, oh you who
weren't around long who
died in the soft mouth of
contemplation oh you who
never met a forest you couldn't
scribble over asking about
waterfalls oh you in the
barrel there

*

the state reproduces itself
by being xeroxed over
and over until all original
traces of the image vanish
but copying remains
sacred, the *act* of xeroxing
revealing our multiplicity, an
endless ritual that lives
on in the architecture
(Alvin Lucier says I am sitting in
a room, over and over, until
his voice becomes the room)

Nadyezhda Tolokonnikova
says the party of the
innocents, Rebekah Rutkoff
says a tiger-eyed opal, a
garnet, an aquamarine,

Jeffrey Jerome Cohen
says the love of stone
is often unrequited

Donna Stonecipher says
room to room in the blue
honeycomb, Alan Felsenthal
says make my soul my
heart's footstool, Julian
Brolaski says brink
ottomat — oddity

Kristen Ross says the extent
to which the insurgents
shared no blueprint, Bob
Dylan says my bell still
rings, Matt Peterson says
we are all crisis actors
                and
maybe that's what we'll
remember, rubber chicken
crisis soft old air inside
a shack crisis the crisis
of infinite opinions

Ishmael Reed says Ringo
crisis enters fifth week,
Sara Larsen says what
I have grave-robbed my
spirit from, Sally Rooney

says a logic submerged
below the level of
equity or argument

(as urgent
as liquid means, Michael
Gizzi said)

and the question of
what survives or doesn't
comes down to
nothing but the attention
of people stuck in time

David Larsen says the
lion and the wolf that
haunt the flock are a
drain on capital, Lucy
Ives says the mind
freed from reason is
full of pictures

in the end all of it
buildings the eradication
of night and whatever
gods became was just
writing conveyed differently
thru differing materials

in the annals of oblivion

there is no place to say
how exuberant were
our diner menus how
we savored the taste of
exile how great it was to
play tetris or ride an
underground rolling
disco to an actual ancient
temple on the edge
of an actual wilderness

or stay up late listening to
records in a small room under
the light of burning filaments

Nathan Austin says we
were bats and we were
angry like bats and like
bats we flapped our
wings and fluttered like
bats, Jalal Toufic says
and it is addressed to
angels

Laura Henriksen
says, do I still have
to tell you that land
isn't wealth to own? no,
everyone knows that

*

we sway in freedom
from the delusion
of permanence,
it's not a harp if it
doesn't bend, (Leslie Scalapino
said individuals both
seeing and creating
the 'conceptual'
interaction that is them)

you can only mourn
things one at a time
you cannot mourn an
entire world at once

Thom Donovan says
sunset of that discourse
this is dawn, Assia Djebar
says it was now the
time for separations

makeshift chorus
pouring meaning into
me as tho I had
a mind to fill, rando
psalmist croons the
lithe accidents of
reading's salvage

in the center of the
glass megaroom a
scale model of before
the fires, we had
feelings about our
phones and lost
our stupid bodies

Anna Gurton-Wachter
says I sleep inside of
convergence where
my two tongues meet,
Suzanne Stein says religio-
spiritual ardor as
a psycho-surgical
maneuver, John Godfrey
says the bus kneels

Robert Kelly says you
can never have the
word of God you can
only speak it,
Simone White says
reaching into intelligibility
with voice for contact,
Alan Davies says reassure
nova memo museum

so capital
unclenches time and

weeks stop happening
"I love you, robot!"
we hear so little of
what we say so little
of we say, where we
touch we go tense, music
pulls, muscles pulse,
under the unraveling
seasons which walk past
a lawyer's office a funeral
home a conch with umbrellas
meat on grills and intermingling
radio a monument to someone
who doesn't know about the
monument a giant bucket of
crabs clockwise and
counter-clockwise turning

postscript to some of the preliminaries

on eighteenth brumaire
in the year of infinite
napoleons america did
the least gnostic thing
               as
tho to test the elastic
that barely holds us plural
to snap every branch burn
honey as tho to rain a
lesson of stones on every
consensus exposed to
sky
    the imperators gather
like the purple of a bruise
or of a toga picta, the
shawl painted purple of
a general in triumph
dyed with shellfish
from phoenicia, the ambit
of force to drain colors
from the sea, and
now they're standing
under a torn canopy
howling the math of
bare dominance, we
know blood will be
on both sides of the skin

that it is already
>	we

love to call what
we're doing a vote
>	tear

up the festival
let the streets go to
hyenas let the air
overhead be nothing
but a swirl of gas
>	we

read a lot about how
social media is dividing
us into homogenous
echo chambers, making
us think ours is the only
opinion, when I ride the
train tho people are
crying all kinds of people
and I don't know them
often don't understand
their languages but
in tunnels underground
I know why they're
crying
>	it reminded

me of how during
occupy you'd sometimes
be on the train &
someone would stand

up & announce hey
I just wanna say
that I'm really happy
about what's happening
on wall street it was
all kinds of people
I didn't know them but I
knew why in tunnels
underground they were
making speeches

   whoever you look
out over the same harbor
as is your country. what
ever hand you find is
for holding. believe the
news it happened. every
body will help you some
people are very kind.

   Rousseau writes
that a new politics is like a
baby, gurgling up
a music of mashed
articulations. not
everything is a demand
sometimes the city wails.
Jakobson writes about a
time in the development
of a baby called

the acme of babble
the baby produces
a never ending stream
of random sounds
this acme is the
moment when the
articulatory palette these
sounds are drawn from
is at its widest from here
the repertoire will
be whittled down to
the sounds of the languages
the baby is acquiring
      Tsvetaeva
to Rilke: keine sprache ist
muttersprache — no tongue
the mother tongue
     god
in deuteronomy: you infuriated
me with a no-god I will
make of you a no-people.
but we didn't sin enough &
never learned to be no
this wrenching yes that's
killing us
    Angela Davis writes
it is interesting how much
more difficult it is to
transform discourses than
it is to build new

institutions.
        the discourse of
no, the makeshift institutions
of no that we will create.
the morning of no the
breakfast of no the classrooms
of no. the purple mountain
majesties of no the stained
toga of no. the no writing on
the wall. the sandbox of
no, city of no, people's
council of no. taxi no. phone
booth no. bookshelf after
bookshelf resounding with
no. ice cream of no &
vegan ice cream of no. we
have no time for atheism.
horizons of no and container
ships of no pumping no
at the no station. let the
no star find you your way
home now that they're
burning maps in the
towers.
    walmart has
a sale on apparatchiks
this week get 'em while
they're hot. I keep wanting
to be funny but I feel
that I shouldn't

                      the ones
who rolled up their
windows against a
bleeding country, who
mistook smugness for
vision, who rolled their
eyes when corruption
made us angry, who
took distraction for their
birthright and shat
on the name of peace
are now licking the
floor for milk.
              we
see each other
underground and
we're all just crying
to know how late it is &
that we too are like all
the others

<u>a note</u>

in addition to recurring language from ancient texts that appears periodically throughout this book, there are numerous quotations from other writers. "full of holes, aching" is from Robert Creeley's "Poem." "poets who carry poetry instead of money" are from Osip Mandelstam's "An Army of Poets." "homesickness for world culture" is a very rough translation of Mandelstam's answer when asked to define "akmeizm." for those interested in the oprichnina, there are many interesting (mostly russian) cultural explorations; I recommend Tchaikovsky's opera "the oprichnik." "the lightfoot hears you and the brightness begins" is the first line of Robert Duncan's "Poem Beginning With a Line by Pindar," from which "the thundermakers descend" and a few lines in that poem are taken. also one from Louis Zukofsky. "bastards came" is Clark Coolidge. "the air & how to fill it" is excerpted from comments Janis Joplin once made about Bessie Smith. "a mountain for president" is the title of a very beautiful song by principles of geometry. "everybody will help you, some people are very kind" is a lyric from Bob Dylan's "I'll Keep It With Mine." "we, too, are like all the others" is an adaptation of Beethoven's retraction of the eroica's dedication to Napoleon. all other borrowings, I think, are marked in the poems themselves. I know some people really like van halen; I do not wish to offend you, but I disagree.

acknowledgments

my supreme gratitude is due to Anna Gurton-Wachter, who has provided a frankly psychedelic amount of moral support, editorial consultation, sustaining buffoonery, & full-spectrum comradeship. I love you.

I am deeply indebted to the wonder-workers of Ugly Duckling Presse, most especially my gracious, perceptive, and inordinately patient editors, Daniel Owen and Lee Norton, and publicist Sarah Lawson. you are all wonderful. several of the poems included here have been previously published in *BOMB*, *Nat. Brut*, and *Elderly*, and I owe a huge debt of editorial thanks to Andrew Bourne, Jennifer Soong, and Nick DeBoer, respectively, for their support and feedback.

my luck in having cover art by noted alien king Andrew Steinmetz is matched only by my luck in our decades of close friendship & bandmatehood.

major shouts-out to: my mom & dad, Sonja & Alan Dreiblatt; my sister Sara and brother Noah; Matthew, Sophia, and Robbie McLaughlin; Lily Gurton-Wachter, Andrew Leland, and Oscar Leland.

fireworks of appreciation to Thom Donovan, Eugene Lim, and Asiya Wadud for reading and providing comment on earlier iterations of this manuscript, and for their profoundly nourishing society. to Peter Dimock, without whose years of friendship and mentorship I can hardly imagine a life or mind for myself. to Nathan Austin, who answered a preposterousness of questions with a generosity that is no less incredible for its being characteristic. to Lewis Freedman, who encouraged the earliest versions of this book to keep breathing.

thank you hugely to Adjua Gargi Nzinga Greaves, at whose invitation I was honored to share some of this work at the poetry project, and with whom I was honored to discuss that reading in great detail retrospectively. more than honored, really, like I fell asleep on the honor train and woke up miles past my stop.

my reading of Rousseau is greatly indebted to conversations with Armando Mastrogiovanni, far more knowledgeable than I, in 2011 in the miraculous tumult of liberty square.

I am far more grateful to the following people than the mere inclusion of their names in a list lets on; I could write a whole book about each of their encouragement and support, various in kind and, to me, unmistakable: Matvei Yankelevich, Jon Woodward, Jared White, Anna Vitale, Michael Varga, Jonathan Valk, Genya Turovskaya, Adam Tobin, Bridget Talone, Mary South, Rebekah Smith, Ada Smailbegovic, Cam Scott, Dave Sargeant, Kate Robinson, Elizabeth Robinson, Simon Reichley, Ted Rees, Moudhy Al-Rashid, Hilary Plum, Jeff Peterson, Anastasiya Osipova, Mark Nowak, JW McCormack (MTFFYF),

Charlotte Mandell, Dan Magers, Gracie Leavitt, Robert Kelly, Taso Karnazes, MC Hyland, Kimberly Lyons, Lauren Levin, David Larsen, Brenda Iijima, Bethany Ides, Jeremy Hoevenaar, Eli Friedman, Farrah Field, Chad Felix, Farnoosh Fathi, Alan Davies, Danny Diamond, Alex Cuff, Julia Chang, Louis Bury, Dror Burstein, Marie Buck, Madeleine Braun, Hayden Bennett. tho I can't imagine she knows it, Catherine Taylor offered a stray encouragement that hugely influenced the writing of this book (please don't hold it against her).

my deep apologies in advance to anyone I've forgotten here. it is really something, being a terrestrial human.